Cambridge English R

Level 3

Series editor: Philip Prowse

The Ironing Man

Colin Campbell

CAMBRIDGE
UNIVERSITY PRESS

CAMBRIDGE UNIVERSITY PRESS
Cambridge, New York, Melbourne, Madrid, Cape Town, Singapore,
São Paulo, Delhi

Cambridge University Press
The Edinburgh Building, Cambridge CB2 8RU, UK

www.cambridge.org
Information on this title: www.cambridge.org/9780521666213

First published 1999
17th printing 2009

Printed in India by Thomson Press

Illustration by Gary Taylor

A catalogue record for this publication is available from the British Library

ISBN 978-0-521-66621-3 paperback
ISBN 978-0-521-68614-3 paperback plus audio CD pack

Contents

Characters

Tom: works in London and lives in a small village outside London

Marina: Tom's wife

Tracy: a beauty consultant and masseuse

Phil: a detective

The Ironing Man

Chapter 1 *The fridge door*

Marina looked at the fridge for a moment and then read out the list of words written on the fridge door:

washing up after a meal
vacuum cleaning
ironing
cleaning
shopping

This was her 'top five'. It was a bit like the 'top ten' on the radio. You know, the best selling records of the week. The only difference was that her 'top five' was actually her 'bottom five'. Let me explain. The thing that was top of her list was actually the thing she hated doing the most.

Sometimes it was very difficult to decide which *one* of the five she really hated the most. Then she might put two things in first place. Or three things. Sometimes she really wanted to put them all in first place. She hated all of them. She hated all kinds of housework. Full stop.

There were just two reasons why she did not put everything in first place. Reason one: the fridge door was not wide enough. Reason two: changing the 'top five' was one of the only things that she enjoyed doing in the kitchen. It gave her the time to make a cup of coffee and drink it slowly, and it gave her time to think. Sometimes she played a game with herself and moved the letters around to make other words, words describing more interesting activities, like:

move out of the village
go back to London
find a job and meet fun-loving people

The idea of the game was to use all the letters on the fridge to make new words. Once she used nearly all of them but then found that the letters she had left spelt out the words:

leave Tom

She put the letters back as they had been. She hated housework but she loved Tom. She did not want to leave him.

Tom and Marina had been married now for almost three years. The first two and a half years in London. Wonderful London. Fun London. Things-to-do and people-to-meet London. TOO-FAR-AWAY-LONDON!! They now lived in a small village called Felton, near Cambridge. They had lived here, in the middle of nowhere land, for ninety-two days and (looking at the clock) four hours, thirty-eight minutes.

She looked again at the fridge door. The letters had little magnets on the back so that when you put them on anything metal they stayed there. Marina thought about what other people did with them. Leave little messages for their husbands and wives, like: 'Dear Bill, Your dinner is in the cooker, *I* am in the West Indies' or 'The cat ran away from home. I have decided to join him.' When Tom had seen the list of words Marina had put on the fridge door he smiled and said:

'So this is your "things to do" list. Good idea.'

And then he added:

'There are two "u"s in "vacuum".'

When she explained to Tom about her 'top five' he thought for a moment. Then he looked sad and put his arm around her.

'Oh, you poor thing. I'm sorry. I know it's difficult for you to get used to living here, but you are not too unhappy, are you? Give it a little time. Maybe you could find something to do. Get a job in the village. Have coffee mornings for the other women. Start playing golf.'

Tom was making another list for her and she soon stopped listening. He enjoyed making lists. Things to do at work. Things to do at home. Things to read. He even made lists of other lists he would like to make when he had more time.

When they could not decide how to spend their bank holidays he would make a list of things they could do. Sometimes he spent the day just making a list of what they could do. By the time he had finished it was too late to go anywhere or do anything. This did not really matter as it always seemed to rain on bank holidays anyway. He made lists of places they could visit. He made lists of restaurants they could stop at on the way to those places. He made lists of things they could eat at those restaurants. Lists of friends they could invite to their house for dinner. This last list was very short. They had no friends in the village. There was no-one of their age in the village. Everyone was older. Even the grandchildren of the people who lived in the village were probably older than they were.

Tom went through his list of things she could do in the village. Marina did not speak. He talked, she listened. He made lists, she listened. But she did think about what he was saying and the lists he made.

Find a job in the village? There was one shop in the village. There was also a café that opened in the summer. Mrs Pringle-Smythe was the manager of both of these places and she didn't seem to need anyone else. Not many people lived in the village and not many people passed through the village and no tourists came to the village. Well, tourists came to the village if they had lost their way. So the shop and the café were not very busy, and there was nowhere else in the village to work.

Coffee mornings? The women in the village probably enjoyed coffee mornings. The women she had met always enjoyed talking about the weather. They got very excited talking about the weather. They often compared the weather now with the weather when they were young, many, many years ago. For example, the women would say:

'Oh, it's not like it used to be. When we were young it was always hot in summer – long, hot, summer days. Do you remember, Susan, how hot it used to be?'

'Of course I do, Sally. And the winters were lovely too, short, cold days. And there was always snow on Christmas Day. But now, well, you never know what the weather's going to be like, do you? It's the end of the world.'

Or the women got sad, and sometimes almost angry as they talked about how the village had changed (and all the changes were bad changes!).

Marina had no idea what they were talking about. Nothing had changed in the village since Tom and Marina had come to live here. Well, that was not quite true. There was a new sign for the National Lottery outside the village shop now. The women were probably thinking about that! Nothing else had changed since Queen Victoria had passed through the village as a young child almost two hundred years ago. (Her driver was new and they had got very lost.)

Start playing golf? For Marina, if there was one thing she did not understand about men, and actually there were many things she did not understand about men, it was why they got so excited running after balls. Little balls, big balls, round balls, not quite round balls, soft balls, hard balls. And when they were tired of running after balls or too old to run, they *walked* slowly after balls. Balls!

She looked again at the fridge door. Poor Tom. He was so busy with his new job that he did not see how bored she was becoming, how unhappy she was.

She put 'ironing' at the top of the list on the fridge. Then she walked over to the ironing board, which stood in the corner of the kitchen. She picked up a shirt and looked at it. She could not remember if she had already ironed this one. She probably had ironed it but it still looked as if someone had been playing football with it.

Balls, she thought, and smiled to herself. She looked at the shirt again.

She remembered once ironing a shirt. First she ironed one side, then she turned it over and ironed the other side.

But when she turned the shirt over again it still looked as if it needed ironing. She probably spent half an hour ironing the same shirt before she realised what she was doing. Now that was her idea of a bad time.

Marina stopped smiling as she remembered this. She looked at the small mountain of clothes on the floor waiting to be ironed. Actually it was not a *small* mountain at all. It was small in the same way that Mount Everest is small. How could two people have so many clothes? And why did they always need ironing? And why, oh why, could she not find someone else to do this boring ironing for her? And who ... and who was that at the door?

Chapter 2   *The Ironing Man*

When the door bell rang Marina did three things. Firstly, she did nothing because no-one ever rang the door bell. No-one came to visit, no-one came at all, so she did not believe it was ringing. Secondly, she put the iron down on top of the shirt she was ironing and looked up. Thirdly, she walked to the door. She walked slowly, carefully and quietly.

She looked through the small hole in the middle of the door. There was someone there. Someone was standing outside her front door. She could not see if it was a man or a woman because the hole was in the middle of the door. She could not see a face but there was definitely someone there. She looked again through the hole and then jumped as the bell rang again.

She tried to remember what to do when this happened. When they had lived in London she had just opened the door and not really thought too much about it. But in London people very often rang the door bell. Here in the village it almost never happened. People did not visit each other, people did not go from house to house selling things. Who could it be? Maybe it was a wrong number. No, wrong numbers were just on the telephone, weren't they?

The door bell rang again. It rang the same way, not more impatient than the last time, not more impatient than the first time. She thought of the film on television she had watched the night before. It was a horror film about dead people who come back to life in a small village:

A young woman is alone in the old dark house on a night when the rain comes down like a river and the wind shakes the trees and the windows. The lights suddenly go out and there is a loud knock at the door, and then another knock, and another, heavier than before. The young woman goes to the door and asks 'Who's there?' in a shaking voice but before the words have left her mouth the door opens and the ...

But this was not a film and it wasn't raining and anyway Marina did not really believe in the 'living dead'. Not in the middle of the day, anyway, when it was light outside. The door bell rang again and this time Marina opened the door.

He was quite tall, good-looking (very good-looking) and he was wearing jeans and a white T-shirt. And he had a smile that you only see at the cinema or on television.

'Hello.'

'Hello.'

'I've come to do the ironing for you,' he said.

Marina smiled at him. Then she stopped smiling and looked at him. Then she smiled at him again and turned her head to one side. Just a little, because she did not want to look away from this face, this smile. Then she stopped smiling again and tried very hard to think of what to say next. Finally it came to her.

'Sorry?'

And then she thought of something else.

'You've come to do *what?*'

The man continued to smile at her and explained.

'You wanted someone to do your ironing for you,' he said. 'You hate doing ironing. You made a wish, remember? About your ironing? That's why I am here.'

The conversation might have continued like this for some time. But suddenly the smell of burning shirt reached them and they both ran into the kitchen.

Chapter 3 *Teddy bears make poor soldiers*

The smell of burning shirt had almost gone already. Most of the smell had gone with the shirt, which the Ironing Man had carried out to the garden.

Marina had acted very quickly when they ran back to the kitchen. She had picked up the goldfish bowl and emptied it over the burning shirt. (She remembered to move the iron away first.) It was not a real goldfish in the bowl. Marina liked animals too much to throw one on top of a burning shirt.

There were other things to throw. Like the mineral water that Tom kept in the fridge. The mineral water Tom kept in the fridge was always the same kind: it was still water, not sparkling; it was Irish, not French; it came in glass bottles, not plastic bottles. Tom knew what he liked, and he never changed the things he liked.

The goldfish, however, was plastic and so Marina did throw him and the water on the burning shirt. As he was a plastic goldfish he did not show any great surprise to find himself lying on the floor. The little key in his side was turning around slowly. If you turned the key a few times and returned the fish to the water, he swam around the bowl. He opened and closed his mouth, trying to take in all the air that plastic goldfish do not actually need.

Marina had bought him in a shop in London as a

present for her nephew. But then she had decided to keep the goldfish herself and he had soon become very important for her. She sometimes stood and watched him swimming round and round. Once, Tom had surprised her in the kitchen watching the goldfish. She was opening and closing her mouth at the same time as the fish, and repeating in a soft voice, 'I know how you feel, I know how you feel, I know how you feel . . .'

So the smell in the kitchen now was not burning shirt but coffee, fresh coffee that she had made for herself slowly and with love. She was now drinking the coffee slowly, enjoying every drop.

The Ironing Man had gone. The shirts were ironed and sitting on the bed, one on top of another. Normally Marina just pushed them into a cupboard beside the bed, happy not to have to look at them any more, happy to see the mountain of clothes disappear into something as small as the cupboard.

But these shirts were so beautifully ironed – they looked just the way they do when you buy them in the shops – that she did not want to put them away in the cupboard. So she left them on the bed where Tom would see them when he came home. He would love it. She looked forward to when he came back.

Tom would not realise that one shirt was missing. He had a lot of shirts and they were all the same. They were all white with a thin blue stripe. All his suits were dark grey and all his jackets were dark blue. All his shoes were black except the ones he used for walking, which were brown. This way of doing things made life easier, as Tom once explained to Marina:

'I get up in the morning, I put on a shirt, I put on a suit, I put on my shoes, and I don't have to think about what I'm doing. I don't have to make decisions about what I am going to wear, because I always wear the same things. It's quick, it's easy and I save so much time.'

Tom was very pleased with this way of getting dressed. He never said anything openly about it, but he really thought Marina should do the same thing. He thought she wasted time. Every day when Marina got up she first had to think about how she was feeling and then decide what blouses and skirts and colours and materials matched those feelings. She wanted her clothes to say something about her and about how she was feeling that day. It took her a long time to get dressed. What a waste of time! But Tom took three minutes to get dressed, every day. Three minutes.

No, Tom would not notice that one white shirt with a blue stripe was missing. Marina did not have to worry about that. She could continue to enjoy 'wasting' more time over this cup of coffee, listening to the piano music on the radio and looking out the window at the garden.

The garden was new, like the house, but there was a difference. The house looked finished. It did not look very interesting. In fact, it looked like all the other twenty-three houses on the street that had been built at the same time. But at least the house did look as if someone had planned it and it did look finished.

The garden did not. No-one had planned this garden. This garden was still waiting for someone to plan it, still waiting for someone with green fingers (you know, someone who is good with plants and flowers). Or maybe it was just waiting for someone with a pair of working hands. Marina and Tom had planted some grass in the garden when they first came to the village, and bits of grass were coming through, here and there, but not, I am sad to say, everywhere.

The garden looked a bit like the beard Tom had tried to grow as a student. Parts of it were really quite good with lots of hair, but other parts had no hair at all. The parts with hair looked like a coconut, and the parts without hair looked a bit like an egg. But, well, eggs and coconuts do not normally go together. So Tom's beard did not really look like a beard, and this garden did not really look like a garden.

Marina saw a butterfly flying in the garden. She was not surprised that the butterfly seemed to be flying straight through the garden, not finding anything beautiful to look at, no flowers to rest on. She loved the way butterflies flew. No straight lines, no hurrying to get somewhere. Up and down and backwards and forwards.

Then the butterfly stopped. He didn't stop in the garden, but he had decided to come and sit on the window and look at Marina. She looked at him sitting on the window, looking in. He moved his wings as if to say hello and when Marina did not answer, the butterfly decided to send a message in code. At least, that is how it seemed to Marina. The butterfly hit the window first with one wing and then with the other as if he really was sending a message.

The problem was that Marina did not understand the code the butterfly was sending. She did not understand any code for sending messages. Sometimes she thought she was not very good at communicating at all in any language. She certainly did not think she was good at communicating with Tom any more.

Once, when she was at school, she had almost learnt Morse code. She had joined a kind of junior army for schoolchildren. Her parents could not believe it.

'You want to be a soldier? You want to play with guns?' her mother asked with a look that Marina knew well. The look said, 'where is the little girl I used to know?'

'I like the uniform, you know, the jacket and the trousers, they are really great,' Marina explained.

'And the boots are nice too,' she added. Her mother still looked as if she did not believe any of this.

'And the boys?' her mother asked, thinking that maybe her fifteen year old daughter was beginning to show an interest in boys, at last.

'Nothing's perfect,' said Marina with a smile.

But she soon had a fight with one of the teachers. They were going on a training exercise and had to carry heavy bags on their backs. Marina's bag was a little heavier than anyone else's.

'Teddy goes everywhere with me,' she answered when the teacher asked her what she was doing with a teddy bear on the top of her bag.

'I'll take care of him,' she continued.

'You will not *take* care of him,' the teacher said. 'You will not *take* him. Anywhere! Do you understand me? This is a serious exercise. It is not for children and training exercises are not a place for toys. I repeat, do you understand me? You look stupid. You will make us all look stupid. And what is most important you will make *me* look stupid.'

Marina did not want to say that the teacher already looked stupid. But it was probably a good time for her, and the bear, to leave the junior army. Even if it meant she never learnt Morse code and could not understand the messages the butterfly was sending.

She reached out to the butterfly. She put her hand on the window and hit her fingers against the window, sending out little messages to the butterfly. They continued like this for some time, fingers and wings knocking against the window, both of them happy to rest there and watch each other for a while.

What did the butterfly think of her, living in this house, living between these four walls? Did he know about the straight lines that people lived along?

school → university → job;
family → friends → boyfriends → husband → children;
room → flat → house → bigger house → bigger house
with garden.

Did the butterfly ask itself why she did not fly like him, here and there and up and down and backwards and forwards, moving where it wanted, when it wanted? Marina looked at the butterfly and asked herself the same questions. Then she remembered something else.

She had read in a newspaper something about an idea that everything in the world is joined together. If you change one thing then this will change other things as well. She remembered the example they talked about. A butterfly lands on a flower somewhere in the east part of the world and this changes something else, and then something else changes and then something else and something else until, finally, there is an earthquake in another part of the world, in the west, thousands of miles away.

Marina looked at the butterfly and asked him:

'What changes will you bring to my life? Will there be an earthquake somewhere in the world because you stopped to visit me today? Will there be an earthquake in my life?'

She smiled at her own thoughts and then opened her hand on her side of the window. She invited the butterfly to come in and sit on her hand. But the butterfly disappeared as the front door opened and Tom came into the house.

At first she was still so lost in her conversation with the butterfly that she did not realise what was happening. But then she did. She realised that Tom was home, and she remembered everything that had happened to her that day: the stranger who had offered to do the ironing and the butterfly who had stopped to talk through the window. That was a lot to happen in one day. She could not remember another day since they had moved to the village when so much had happened.

Everything came back to her suddenly and like a child (like the child she was still happy to be, like the child most of us have forgotten we ever were), she ran towards the door, jumping from one foot to another. She ran to tell Tom everything, to share it all with Tom.

She didn't think for a moment that there was anything strange about her day. Not a thought. Her only thought was to tell him all about it. After all, things do not seem real until we tell someone else about them, do they? And Marina wanted this day to be real. And so she told Tom. She told him everything.

Chapter 4   *Good 7 Bad 1*

The next morning, after Marina had told Tom everything about her day, Tom made his usual trip to work in London. He drove to Cambridge station and found a table all to himself on the 8.35 train to London. He was worried that someone would arrive and sit opposite. This would leave Tom no room for his mobile phone, his laptop computer and his *Financial Times*, or his cappuccino from the French Café at the station.

But then the train left the station and he could relax. A table all to himself. This *was* a good start to the day. He should write this down immediately. He took out the small notebook he kept in his jacket pocket and opened it.

This was his 'Good and Bad book'. In this book he wrote down all the good and all the bad things that happened to him every day of his life. At the end of the day he could see what kind of day it really had been. If there were more good things than bad things, it was a good day. If there were more bad than good things, it was a bad day. Easy. Before he was married, a girlfriend had once asked him:

'What happens if you have one good thing and seven bad things, but the one good thing is really wonderful, and the seven bad things are really not important? Wouldn't that be a good day then?'

Tom had thought about that for a while, but not for too long. He really did not think he would be with this girlfriend much longer anyway, so he did not want to waste time.

'That would make it too difficult,' he said, 'and anyway, if something wonderful happens to you then everything you do that day is wonderful. So you write down lots more good things, because everything seems good to you. Like when you are in love, you know, and everything seems wonderful.'

He had sat back and smiled when he said that. He was pleased with his answer. He liked the middle part of his answer. He thought it was very intelligent. He thought it might even be true, which was another good thing. He was not so happy about the last part. When he had started talking about love he realised that his girlfriend began to smile at him. It was a really wide and open smile and then she took his hand. She looked at him with eyes that were impossibly big and said, 'Oh Tom!' She thought he was talking about them! About him and her, about them being in love.

Tom shook his head as he remembered all this. The picture of his girlfriend's face disappeared. Well, they had stopped going out soon after that. They just did not understand each other.

He came back to the present and looked at his notebook. He wrote the date at the top of an empty page and drew a big thick line down the middle of the page from top to bottom. On the left side he wrote 'Good' at the top of the page and on the other side he wrote 'Bad'. Then he wrote:

seat and table to myself on 8.35 train to London.

Under 'Good', of course. He smiled, looked out of the window, smiled again and then looked back at the notebook at what he had written the day before.

There were seven things under 'Good' and only one thing under 'Bad'.

He looked at them.

Good

1 Found a good place to park the car
2 Finished my report
3 Gave my report to the boss BEFORE BRIAN DID!!!
4 Boss laughed at my joke
    (It was a joke that Tom's nephew told him, but it was one of the ten year old's more adult jokes.)
5 Showed the boss how to use the new photocopier
6 Got a new phone with three lines
7 Boss left office before me and said 'working late, Tom. Good man' (with a smile!)

What a day! What a day!
He looked at the bad column.

Bad

1 Marina?????????

He had written this late last night. He had not had time to write any more than this. He had not really understood what was going on. He had wanted to sleep on it. Think about it. That had not helped. Well, it had helped a little because he had forgotten about it when he was sleeping.

And until this moment he had still forgotten about it, but now it was coming back and it felt like . . . how did it feel? It felt like someone had thrown a big bowl of very cold water over him, on a hot day, when he was not expecting it, when he was looking somewhere else. That is how it felt as he remembered last night and the conversation he had had with Marina, or rather, what Marina had talked to him about, because Tom had said very little.

He went over the conversation again in his head. The way he understood it, of course.

'Hi Marina, how are you?'

'Hi Tom. Have a good day?'

'Yeah, so-so.' (He had not had time then to check his notebook so he did not tell her what a good day it actually had been.)

And then he had asked her about hers, the way you do, you know, like this:

'What about you? How was your day?'

Well, you ask these things but, of course, what you expect to hear is, 'Yeah, fine,' or ,'Yeah, OK,' or ,'Yeah, so-so,' and that is usually it. You can go on and do something else. Change your clothes, take a shower, put your feet up, turn the television on, maybe even open a beer, if it has been a really good day. Or open a beer if it has been a really bad day. You do not expect this kind of answer:

'WONDERFUL!!! GREAT!!! I've had a wonderful day. You won't believe it!'

She had said it exactly like that, in capital letters: (G-R-E-A-T) and with exclamation marks (!!!).

She then told him a story about a man who had come to the house, done the ironing for her and had stayed a while to talk to her and drink a coffee with her. This man did not give his name and did not explain how he knew she was doing the ironing. He did not ask for any money or give her any other information about who he worked for or anything. It was mad. Tom could not understand it. It did not make any sense.

Secondly, Marina had told Tom about a conversation she had had with a butterfly. OK, she had told this story with a smile and a laugh, but it still seemed strange to Tom. Tom did not use a lot of words and did not easily share them with anyone. Least of all with animals.

Finally, when Tom had gone very quiet, Marina told him that she was going up to London on Thursday to meet a friend. When Tom had asked who she was going to meet she had not answered at first and then she said 'Joanne'.

Tom had asked, 'Joanne Searle?' because this was the only Joanne they knew and Marina had replied, 'Yes, isn't that nice. She phoned me, a total surprise.'

A total surprise was right. Tom knew Joanne. He had worked with her in London for three years. But he also knew, as Marina clearly did not know, that Joanne had given up her job six months ago and had gone to live with a group of Buddhists in Nepal.

'I've had enough of running around trying to get somewhere,' Joanne had told him before leaving for Nepal. 'Because when you get there you can't remember why you wanted to be there in the first place. I'm going to learn to be happy being who I am, and where I am!'

Joanne was going to spend three years, three months and three days learning how to meditate. She had not organised a going away party and clearly Marina did not even know she had gone away.

Tom looked out of the window of the train for a moment and then looked back at his list of bad things and wrote some more notes under 'Marina?' Like this:

Ironing Man
butterfly
Joanne

Then he wrote:
Is Marina going mad? Is my wife seeing another man?
Maybe yesterday had not been such a good day after all.

Chapter 5 *Strangers on a train*

Tom was still sitting on the train when his mobile phone rang. Someone from his office. He answered it. His mobile phone rang again. Someone from the office again. He answered it. His mobile phone rang again. Someone from the mobile phone company asking if he was happy with his mobile phone. Normally Tom loved his mobile phone. He could be in touch with the world at any time. If he was out of the office he could tell them where he was and what he was doing. Even if his boss could not see him, Tom could always talk to him. Tom remembered his mother saying that 'little children should be seen but not heard'. But Tom knew that to get anywhere in business you either had to be seen or heard all the time. Usually both.

Now, however, he was not so happy with his mobile phone. He was trying to think. He was trying to think about Marina and the phone calls were making it impossible to think.

He went to the toilet. He did not need to go, but he had found out on his last train journey that, for some reason he did not understand, his mobile phone did not work in the toilet. He had discovered this because he had walked into the toilet with his mobile in his hand, talking to someone (not his boss, thank God!) and the phone stopped working the minute he got inside and closed the door. Tom had thought the train was in a tunnel. He had looked out of the little window they have in train toilets, the one that looks like there is ice all over it, but they were not in a tunnel. He tried to phone the person back but his phone would not work. Then the moment he stepped out of the toilet, the phone rang.

So Tom went to the toilet so he would have time to think. On his way there he suddenly remembered how his father used to spend hours in the toilet when Tom was a child. Maybe his father had also been looking for somewhere to think.

And so he sat and the phone did not ring and he tried to think but he could not get any further than:

Ironing Man	Is Marina going mad? Is my wife seeing another man?
butterfly	going mad?
Joanne Searle	another man?

Why would Marina say she was going to meet Joanne in London if Joanne was in Nepal? Who was she going to meet? If something was going on between her and this Ironing Man person would she tell Tom about it? Well, maybe she was not sure if she was going to go out with this man or not. Maybe she just wanted to see what Tom would say or do when he heard the story. (Tom had said and done very little when he heard the story.) Maybe she was just going mad because she was so bored at home in the village. What was she going to do in London? That was the question!

This question was still going around in Tom's head as he returned to his seat.

Tom was not very happy when he saw that a man was now sitting on the other side of the table. Tom could not see his face because the man was reading a newspaper and was holding the newspaper in front of him. Tom sat down and looked at the back page of the newspaper. The man went on reading. Tom did not like this newspaper. Tom did not think it was a *news*paper at all. What news? The paper was full of big photographs, big headlines, big ... well, big everything, as if the readers had forgotten their glasses or were just learning to read.

At university Tom and his friends used to play a game in groups with this newspaper. Each group had three minutes to read the newspaper and then another person would ask both the groups questions about what was in it. The groups with men always remembered the name of the girl on page three! There was always a girl on page three and she was almost never fully dressed. And men always seemed to remember her name. But then in three minutes you could actually read all of this newspaper from the front page to the back page and still have time to look at the photograph of the girl on page three, and then look at her again, and perhaps again.

So Tom very quickly got bored reading the back page of the newspaper. He did not, however, feel like working. He noticed another newspaper lying on the table in front of him. The man had clearly brought this one as well. It was his village newspaper which Tom did not normally read because it was so boring. It always had stories about people getting married and stories about lost cats and the problem of ducks from the village crossing the main road to get to a river on the other side of the road. The headline read:

SAVE OUR DUCKS – BUILD BRIDGE

There were a lot of headlines like that in the village newspaper. But, maybe it was better to read a newspaper and not think about Marina. Not think at all. The man was still reading the other newspaper, so Tom looked through the village paper quickly, hoping to find something of interest. Not a lot! Something about a bank manager who had lost all his hair and had now asked the bank workers to shout at him as often as possible. The manager had read somewhere that this might make his hair grow again. Something about the village school sports day. Something about a man who had grown the biggest cucumber in England (second biggest in the world), but his wife had still left him.

Tom looked up at the man across the table, but the man was still reading the newspaper, still holding it in front of him. He did not seem to have turned a page since Tom had sat down. Was he sleeping? A slow reader? No-one could read that slowly!

Tom went back to the village newspaper and started looking through the small advertisements. Advertisements for houses, advertisements for cars, advertisements for different kinds of services. Suddenly one advertisement jumped off the page at Tom.

DO YOU KNOW WHERE YOUR WIFE/HUSBAND REALLY IS WHEN THEY SAY THEY ARE JUST VISITING A FRIEND?
ARE YOU WORRIED THAT MAYBE THEY HAVE FOUND SOMEONE ELSE?

Tom could not believe it. The questions in the advertisement were the same questions he had been asking himself about Marina. It was as if the advertisement was speaking directly to him. He looked again at the advertisement. It was for a private detective. There was a phone number (a mobile phone number) and a promise.

BRING ME YOUR PROBLEMS AND I WILL GIVE YOU ANSWERS ... FAST! AND NO-ONE ELSE WILL EVER KNOW!

The idea of using a private detective had never entered Tom's head. He had seen private detectives on television, usually American ones, usually in California. But private detectives in England? Advertisements for private detectives in Tom's village newspaper, beside the story about the ducks crossing the road? It did not seem possible, but ... maybe this was the way of finding out what was going on with Marina. Maybe this was the way of finding out who she was going to meet in London!

Tom put the newspaper down and put a line under the phone number with his pen, picked up his phone and rang the number. Almost immediately he heard another phone ring, but for some strange reason he could hear it ringing in both his ears. He moved the phone away from his ear but could still hear it ringing. He could hear it ringing through his own phone and from behind the newspaper of the man sitting opposite him. The man opposite put his newspaper down and looked at Tom.

'I see you have found my advertisement,' he said with a big smile.

Chapter 6 *Massage and message*

Marina sat looking at the letters on the fridge door. The letters clearly spelt out the word 'London' but she had no idea who had moved the letters around to make this word. She had not moved the letters, not since the day the Ironing Man came.

She had seen the word when she was talking to Tom, telling him about her day. Tom had not seemed very interested in the story of her day and had been very quiet as she had told him all about the Ironing Man and the butterfly. He had even looked away from her as she told the story. And then she had looked away from him and had seen the word 'London' on the fridge door. So, suddenly, she had told him she was going up to London to see a friend on Thursday. She had no idea where the idea came from, but even as she said it she got very excited about it.

Why did she say she was visiting someone called 'Joanne'? She did not really know. Of course. Joanne was the name of their friend. When Tom said Joanne Searle's name Marina had agreed with him. And that was it. Marina was going to London to see 'Joanne' on Thursday.

And now it *was* Thursday and Marina was sitting at home, looking at the fridge door with no idea of what she was going to do ...

Marina was so excited about going up to London she had not slept well. It was only when she got up in the morning that she realised that she had no plans to go anywhere, that the idea of London had come from nowhere, and that nowhere was probably where she was going today.

She felt very empty now that the chance of getting away from the village, from the house and from the housework for a day had disappeared. She put her hands around the back of her neck. This made her feel a little better. When she had been a child her mother had always touched Marina's back and neck when she was feeling sad. It always made her feel better. She loved to be touched. Even the touch of her own hands made her feel better, but someone else touching her, someone giving her a massage, oh, that was wonderful, that was the most wonderful thing in the world. Well, one of the most wonderful things in the world.

The door bell rang and Marina ran to answer it. She was hoping that the Ironing Man had come back, but it was a woman who stood there. A young woman, about her own age with blonde hair like her own, and a big smile.

'I know you have no idea who I am,' the woman said. 'My name's Tracy. I am a beauty consultant and masseuse. Your friend phoned me and asked me to come and give you a surprise massage.'

Marina laughed out loud.

'You know who phoned me then?' the woman asked.

'I think so. Did he give a name?' Marina asked.

'The Ironing Man? I'm sure *you* know what that means,' and she laughed again. 'I like a man with a bit of iron in him too!'

They laughed together as they walked into the living room. Tracy quickly put up the massage table she had brought with her.

'Is this table safe?' asked Marina.

'I haven't killed anyone yet,' Tracy laughed.

Tracy took some little candles from her bag and lit them. They gave off a sweet smell of flowers.

'Would you like some music? I have some CDs with me, to help you relax.'

'Please.'

Tracy found the CD player and soon the room was full of the sounds of Brazilian rain forests.

'Better than travel,' Tracy joked. 'Well, cheaper anyway.'

The music, and the smell of the candles, and the light touch of Tracy worked their magic on Marina and she was soon travelling. Pictures of holiday places she had visited with Tom came back to her now . . . walks along the empty beaches on that small Greek island at sunset . . . the journey in Egypt over the hills on the backs of donkeys and down to the Valley of Kings . . . sitting on Croagh Patrick, the mountain in Ireland which looks over the Atlantic, where Saint Patrick had spent thirty days and nights alone . . .

The smells and the sounds in the room seemed to change as she travelled from place to place in her thoughts. She smiled to herself with eyes closed and was still smiling some time later when she realised that Tracy had finished her massage. Marina remembered where she was, but she did not want to open her eyes to see it. She wanted to hold on to the smells and sounds from other places, to the pictures of her and Tom in those beautiful places, and to the touch of Tom from other times.

Finally she opened her eyes and saw Tracy smiling down at her.

'How was that?' Tracy asked.

'Wonderful,' Marina replied.

'Told you it was like travelling. Almost as good as sex,' and Tracy laughed again.

They sat for a while over a cup of tea and Tracy gave Marina some of her life story.

'Yeah, I was married for a while. You know, usual story. Boyfriend from school. The first and only boyfriend. I didn't know any better, I thought love was all about giving. Giving flowers and chocolates and having time for each other and looking into each other's eyes for hours and never looking at your watch.

'So, anyway, we got married and went on holiday to the West Indies. That was good too, that was wonderful, but after that, it was never the same again. End of giving, end of having time only for each other. End of all the little surprises. He thought that after we were married he didn't have to do that any more. He thought he didn't have to work at it any more. No more surprises. The only surprise was when he actually listened to what I was saying, or when he didn't look at his watch when I was trying to talk to him.

'It's like all those love stories you read, or see at the cinema, you know, they always seem to end when the man and woman finally get together. Those stories always stop the day they get married. I sometimes think it's men who actually write those stories, not women, you know. And men don't think about what happens after you get married. And maybe women don't either. I didn't. I had no idea what was going to happen next. And my man, he didn't know what to do next, so he just did what his father had done. He went out, earned money, came home, watched television, went out again to the pub with his friends.

Suddenly his idea of a good time seemed to be any time he spent without me.'

Tracy looked sad and thoughtful for a moment, but then her smile and her laugh returned.

'Anyway, I gave him the push after a while. I told him to leave. Best thing I ever did. And now I do things differently. I mean, one day I might find a man who understands you have to go on working on the love after you get married. I mean there must be men like that, somewhere, don't you think? But at the moment what I do is this. I just keep them for a little while. I meet them, they love me, they think I'm wonderful, they think the sun shines out of my eyes, they give me their time and they give me wonderful presents. But, when I see they aren't romantic anymore, then I just let them go. I mean, if men can't take love seriously then why should we take them seriously? Just use them and lose them.'

She laughed again and Marina laughed with her. It was the kind of laugh that invited you to laugh with her.

'I mean, the man I've got at the moment,' Tracy continued. 'He's still in love with me. He brought me here this morning and he is picking me up later and taking me out for the day. For a day of surprises. He has taken the day off work to spend it with me. Can you believe it? No reason. He just wants to spend the day with me. Give him another few months and all the surprises will go. But he'll go as well then. Life's too short, love. Know what I mean?'

Marina nodded her head. Yes, she knew what Tracy meant.

'Your Ironing Man is still romantic anyway, isn't he? Enjoy it while it's there, love,' Tracy said.

The door bell rang. Tracy looked out the window. A man was standing beside a car.

'It's my boyfriend,' Tracy said. 'My day of surprises begins! Oh, he is lovely, though, isn't he? Look at those shoulders, that bottom,' Tracy said. 'So strong! Just looking at him sometimes makes me shake, know what I mean? We can't live without that, can we?'

Marina was not sure if Tracy was talking about sex or not. If she was, Marina was not so sure. It was certainly possible to live without sex for some time. Even for quite a long time. It was Tom's birthday, wasn't it? That was the last time. A month ago! Twenty-nine years old and she was having regular sex. Regular sex once a month! Maybe it was time she took a lover. The thought surprised her and so did Tracy when she spoke.

'Oh my God, I almost forgot,' Tracy said. 'I have a message from the Ironing Man. Your man of iron. He says he'll meet you in the National Gallery at two o'clock this afternoon. Where's that then? In your favourite room, he said. You know what that means, do you? I don't like paintings myself. Well, maybe paintings of men. With no clothes on, of course,' and she laughed her laugh again. 'You'd better hurry up, love, it's almost twelve now!'

Tracy ran out the door and kissed her man. Then he came into the house and took Tracy's bags to the car.

Marina smiled again and then looked at her watch. Tracy was right, she would have to hurry. She ran up the stairs, jumping two stairs at a time. She could not remember ever moving this fast in this house. She did not hear Tracy's boyfriend drive off. She certainly did not hear the second car start and drive off after them.

*　*　*

The detective smiled to himself. 'Good timing,' he thought. He had arrived only ten minutes earlier. He had had trouble finding the house. Well, he did not need to tell Tom he had trouble. All these houses looked the same anyway. But he had time to check the number of the house, and the garden looked just the way Tom had described it – 'like a young man's beard'. The detective had parked his car a few houses away and turned on the little cassette recorder he had bought that morning. He spoke into it.

'I am now outside the house at . . .'

He looked at the cassette. It was not moving. He hit it with his large hand. It still did not move. He wanted to look inside the recorder but his fingers were too thick and he could not open the back of the machine. He looked at it sadly. He never had any luck with machines. He looked at it again and then threw it onto the back seat of the car.

'I'll use a pen and paper,' he said in a loud and angry voice, as if he was speaking to the cassette recorder.

He started to make notes but at that moment he saw that a car was stopping outside the house and, as he watched, a young, good-looking man got out.

'No time to make notes now,' he said to himself, throwing the pen and the notebook onto the back seat of the car to join the cassette recorder.

The detective watched the young woman come to the door. He remembered the notes he had made when he was talking to Tom. Where were they? Of course, in the notebook. He turned round in the car to get the notebook from the back seat. This was not easy because he was a big man and it was a small car. It took a little time and by the time he had got the book the woman was walking with the man towards their car. Carrying two bags. Interesting.

They stopped and the woman put her hand around the man's head and pulled him into a long kiss. Very interesting. The detective looked at his notes again. Young, twenty-nine years old, slim, blonde. Yes, no mistake, this was Tom's wife, this was Marina. The man put the bags into the car, the young woman turned and looked at the house and seemed to wave goodbye to it. Then she turned and kissed the man again as he helped her into the car.

'Very, very interesting,' thought the detective as he started the engine of his car and followed the car with Tom's wife in it down the street.

Chapter 7 *It's just a painting*

Marina arrived at the National Gallery in London and went straight to the room where her favourite painting was. When Tracy had given her the message about the favourite room Marina knew immediately where she meant. The painting was one that Tom had brought her to see on one of their early dates. A favourite painting of his, it quickly became a favourite of theirs.

Marina stood in front of the painting now and looked up at it. The painting was of a woman standing in a room. It could be a kitchen, it could be a living room. A white room with not much furniture but with a beautiful light coming in through the window above and behind the woman. The light falls on the back of the woman's head. She is in her mid-twenties, blonde, with her hair tied up behind her head in a white scarf. She is clearly going to have a baby soon. She is holding a letter in one hand and the second hand rests on her stomach. She is reading the letter and there is a quiet smile on her face as she reads. It is a wonderfully calm painting because of the light, the stillness of the woman, and her smile.

Tom and Marina had sat in front of this painting for twenty minutes when they first came to see it.

'What do you think?' he had asked.

'It's beautiful,' she had replied.

In those days they could sit together for twenty minutes or even longer without saying anything to each other and yet still feel very close to each other.

On their first dates Tom had talked so much that there was never any quiet time between them. He had wanted her to see that he was a nice man, that he was funny and intelligent, so he talked and talked, about himself. But she had wanted him to ask her questions, to show that he was interested in her and not only in himself. It did not happen. Tom gave her his full life story, or the good parts anyway. And he even told her about his earlier girlfriends, saying what had gone wrong, what he had done wrong. But there were no questions, and there were no quiet moments.

Later, as their love developed, they could be quiet together. Looking at each other, looking at a painting, looking at the sea, looking at children playing in the park. They could be quiet and yet be with each other, feel very close to each other.

We sometimes use words to build a wall around ourselves, and sometimes saying nothing can be a way of letting people come really close to us. So in those days when Tom and Marina said nothing to each other, their silence spoke of their love for each other.

Now there was not so much silence between them. She spoke and he made noises to show he was listening. They were usually little noises and she thought that sometimes he was thinking of something else. They were not noises that invited her to say more. There was little of that old quietness.

There was quietness in the painting too, just the woman reading her letter.

'Who do you think the letter's from?' Tom asked.

'Her man,' Marina said.

Tom and Marina had once played a game with Tom's nephew, Rob, in front of this painting. Rob was ten years old and loved to be with them because they were adults who liked to play games and who did not talk to him as if he were a child. In the game they each had to say who they thought the letter was from and what it said.

'Her husband.'

'Her son's school report.'

'It's from her doctor, she has to come to the hospital for a check-up.'

The winner was the person who had the most ideas. Tom won, of course, although Marina and Rob did not like some of his ideas.

'A chance to win World Cup tickets.'

'A letter from her old lover.'

'A bill from her garage.'

'A "Dear John" letter.'

Rob did not understand this. Tom explained:

'It was during the war. It was the kind of letter that some soldiers got when they had been away from home for a long time. A letter from their girlfriends saying, "Dear John, I have found someone else." They called them "Dear John" letters.'

'But she's a woman,' Rob said.

'OK, maybe she's just written a "Dear John" letter and she's reading it again to check for spelling mistakes. They didn't have computers with spell checks then, you know.'

'No, no,' Marina said, and laughed. 'He's away, you're right, that part is true. But it's like this. It's from her husband and he's away looking for a present to give her when the baby is born. He wants to find something that no man has ever given a woman before. He's travelled around Europe and is now in Africa. He's writing to tell her he has found something almost as beautiful as she is, almost as beautiful as the light that came into their bedroom the first morning they lay in bed together as a married couple. And he says that he will be back home soon. And that even though he is far away, when she reads this letter it will be as if he is there with her. And that soon they will lie together again in that beautiful light.'

Tom sat and looked at Marina, his mouth and eyes wide open. His eyes were the size of dinner plates and he said, 'Wow!'

Rob too, although he made a joke about shopping for presents being easier now with the Internet, was looking at Marina with wide eyes and probably thinking something like 'I want to marry you'.

'Don't even think about it!' Tom said to his nephew, reading the look on his face.

Yes, this was an important painting for Tom and Marina. They came back to it now and again, just to check on their feelings for each other. They had not been to see the painting for over a year.

'You're right,' a voice said behind her back. She knew it was the Ironing Man. 'It is from her husband, and it is a letter of love. But, come with me. I want to show you another painting.'

The Ironing Man took her by the hand and they walked

through the gallery, from room to room, slowly moving from one century of paintings to another. He knew where he was going.

Finally they stopped in front of a large painting. It was not an old painting but it told an old story. There were three people in the painting. In the middle was a man dressed in expensive clothes, looking out from the painting, looking important, holding his head high, smiling with a look that says, 'I have everything now'.

In front of him there is another person. It's difficult to tell if it is a man or woman. This person is dressed in white and is not looking at the man. He is looking behind the rich man. There are big houses, expensive cars, beautiful women everywhere. Everything is expensive, everything says this man is rich, this man is important. This man has the world in his hands. But the person in white looks sad.

'What is it?' Marina asked.

'What do you think?'

Marina looked again at the painting. She now saw a third person in the painting, standing behind the smiling rich man, almost completely in the dark. He is also smiling, but it is not a friendly smile. It is a smile that says, 'What you have is nothing. I will come for you and you can do nothing to stop me. Your money will not help you. No-one will be able to help you when I come for you. I will come for you as I will come for all men.'

'This third person is death?' Marina asked.

The Ironing Man nodded.

'And the person in white . . .' Marina thought a little and then turned and smiled at the Ironing Man.

'I think the person in white is like you,' she said. 'I think he has given the man in the painting three wishes, and I think the man has asked for money and . . . and all these cars and houses and things.' She looked back at the painting.

'But now death has come for the man and all of these things mean nothing.'

The Ironing Man smiled at Marina.

'And you have already given me two wishes,' Marina said. 'The Ironing Man and the massage. And I have one more wish?'

The Ironing Man nodded again.

'And you want me to think carefully about it?' she added.

He nodded again and she thought some more.

'And if I asked you to bring Tom back to me,' Marina said. 'To make it like it used to be between us, to make it like it was when we used to sit here and look at the painting of the lady and the letter. Could you do that?'

'And then what would happen?' asked the Ironing Man. 'What has happened between you? If you and Tom were closer again, maybe the same thing would just happen again. What do you want, Marina? What do you really want?'

'I want Tom and me to work hard at making our love grow and continue to grow,' Marina said. 'I know we can do it. I think we have just lost our way a bit. I love him and I know he loves me, but we have forgotten how to work at it. Can you give me that?'

'You have to do that yourself,' the Ironing Man said. 'But maybe I could give you both some time together, a little holiday perhaps. And maybe I can help Tom remember just how much you mean to him, how much he really loves you.'

'*Could* you do that?' Marina asked.

'I think I already have . . .' The Ironing Man thought for a moment and then continued. 'I think I have already started something. I think something may already be happening.'

He smiled at Marina and she smiled back.

'I am sure you can do it, Mr Ironing Man,' she said.

And then she thought of something and her smile disappeared. She looked at him with a question.

'But, that will be four wishes, won't it?' she asked. 'You will help Tom to remember *and* give us time to ourselves? Do I get four wishes?'

'You know, Marina,' said the Ironing Man, 'everything is going up these days. The price of everything is going up, even the number of wishes you get is going up!'

Marina laughed again and looked at him.

'Can I buy you a drink?' she asked.

He shook his head slowly.

'You people . . . I mean you . . . you don't drink, you can't . . .' Marina said slowly.

'No, it's not that,' the Ironing Man said. 'I just thought dinner was probably a better idea. I'll pay, but you choose the restaurant. Italian, I think. That's *my* wish!'

Chapter 8　*The detective reports*

Tom was leaving the office when his mobile phone rang. He looked at it and then turned and looked at the office building behind him. He could not believe it. The only people who phoned him on his mobile were people from work. He was just leaving work and they were phoning him already! He thought about not answering it. Marina did not like the mobile phone for some reason. She had only phoned him once on it, when she had locked herself out of the house without the key. But perhaps it was her. He answered it.

'Hello, is that Dr Watson?' a voice asked.

Tom knew at once it was the detective. The detective had said it was better not to use their real names when they talked on the phone.

'You can never be too careful on the phone,' the detective had said. 'You never know who might be listening.'

Tom thought this was all a bit childish. But the detective seemed hurt when he had said this and so Tom had agreed not to use their real names.

'Yes, this is Watson and you are Mr Holmes?' Tom said.

'I am ready to make my report,' the detective replied.

'What, now? On the phone?' Tom asked.

'No, we should meet. I'd rather do this face-to-face,' the detective said. 'Anyway you have to give me some money for my costs. Your wife has expensive tastes.'

'What do you mean? Where did she go? What did she do? Did she . . . ?' Tom asked.

'All in good time, Dr Watson, but not on the phone,' the detective replied.

'Well, I'm just on my way home,' Tom said.

'I know.'

'How do you know?' Tom asked.

'I can see you from the phone box,' the detective said.

'The phone box?'

'Yes, the phone box,' the detective said. 'My mobile phone isn't working. I've had a bad day with machines, I can tell you, so I had to use a phone box.'

'What are you talking about? What phone box?' Tom asked.

'Behind you,' the detective replied.

Tom turned round. There, standing in a phone box a few metres away, was the detective. He was still wearing his heavy, dirty, white raincoat although it was a warm day. The detective waved at him with his free hand. Well, it was not totally free. He was holding a fat cigar in this hand. A heavy, dirty white raincoat and a cigar? Tom had seen this before somewhere, but he could not remember where. On television? He asked himself where this detective had learnt his job. He wanted to ask him if detectives went to schools, or if they just watched lots of American films. But not now. He listened to the phone and the detective's question.

'Where can we meet?' the detective asked.

'Well, this might seem like a stupid idea, but why don't you come out of the telephone box and we can meet here and now,' Tom answered.

'No, someone might see us together,' the detective said.

'Who? So what if someone sees us?' Tom said.

'Better to be careful,' the detective replied. 'You never know who might be watching.'

Tom began to wonder if all detectives were as strange as this one. Maybe it came with the job. Then he suddenly remembered that he wanted to know what Marina had done in London. What did the detective mean when he said Marina had expensive tastes? He wanted the detective to say that she had come up to London for the day, had not met anyone and had gone back home, happy at the thought of seeing him again. That is what he wanted the detective to say, or something like that.

But that is not what the detective said.

Tom and the detective sat down with their drinks in a quiet pub. Well, actually it was not quiet, the music was playing very loudly even though the pub was empty. Not surprising it was empty, with that noise going on.

'It's good. No-one will hear our conversation,' the detective shouted.

Tom shouted back 'sorry' a few times and then told the detective that the important thing was that they could hear each other, and not that no-one else could hear them. 'Anyway,' said Tom, 'as the pub is empty I don't think anyone can listen to our conversation.' He asked the barman to turn the music off. The barman was not happy to do this.

'People like music when they come to the pub,' the barman said.

'We are the only people in the pub and we don't like it,' replied Tom.

The barman turned the music down, not off, but down.

A little, not a lot, just a little. At least it was possible for Tom and the detective to hear each other. The detective began his report, reading from his notebook.

'I parked my car outside number 35 Greater Blackbird Drive at 11.27 this morning and, after waiting for ten minutes, I saw a car stop outside the above house, 35 Greater Blackbird Drive, and I watched as the woman in question came to the door and . . .'

Tom stopped him. ' "Woman in question?" You mean Marina? Listen, can we do this in English, please? Anyway . . . what car?'

The detective looked a bit hurt. He thought this was how detectives should speak when they give their reports, but Tom clearly did not agree.

'OK,' the detective said. 'Your wife came to the door and kissed the man who had driven up in the car.'

'What? What man? What car?' Tom asked. 'How did she kiss him? Are you sure it was Marina?'

'My dear Watson,' the detective smiled at him as if Tom was a child, 'if you are going to ask me questions now I will never finish this report. Please listen and ask me any questions when I have finished. I think things will become clearer as I continue. OK?'

'All right, but please stop calling me Watson. Where did you get these names from anyway?'

The detective looked hurt again but continued.

'OK,' he said. 'The woman in question . . . sorry, your wife then returned, sorry, she went back into the house and came out with the man and they were carrying two large bags.'

'What!' 'Where was she? . . . Where were they? . . . Was she leaving? . . .'

He did not finish his questions. He did not want to complete his thoughts, thoughts like 'she's leaving me'. Also the detective was now looking at him the way Tom's teachers used to look at him when he was much younger. Tom was older now but the look on the detective's face still stopped him speaking.

The detective continued. 'Your wife and the man then drove off together in the car, a red Volkswagen Golf, the car number was P237 SIM and . . . they took the A14 and drove towards Boddington village . . .'

'I don't want to know the number of the road,' Tom almost shouted. 'I don't want to know the number of the car. I don't care what colour it was, I just want to know what they did, OK?'

'OK, OK,' the detective said. 'They drove to the sports centre. They played tennis. Not very seriously. A lot of laughing. I watched but I couldn't see who won. Not my game anyway, I prefer football. Do you play yourself?'

'Can you please tell me what happened and maybe we can talk about football later?' Tom said.

The detective looked down at his notebook and continued. 'Then they went to lunch. That's what I meant about expensive tastes. An expensive Italian restaurant. And I didn't have much money with me so all I had was a plate of spaghetti and a glass of water. You don't want to know what *they* ate, do you?'

Tom shook his head. He did not know that Marina liked tennis and he did not know that there were any good restaurants near them at all. The last time they had eaten out was on his birthday, in a pub. They had gone home and made love. My God, that was the last time they had made love. Four weeks ago?

'Well, they didn't seem very interested in what they were eating either, you know, more looking into each other's eyes than looking at the plate, if you know what I mean,' the detective said.

Now it was Tom who used a look on the detective. The detective coughed, said 'sorry' and continued.

'Then they drove down to the coast. One hundred kilometres! Can you believe it? And all they did when they got there was walk along the beach for ten minutes, take off their shoes, walk into the sea, kiss each other for, I don't know, probably five minutes, and the beach was really wet, look at my shoes! ... And then they looked at each other and said something, I couldn't hear what they said. I mean, I was actually quite close to them but they didn't see me. I don't think they would have seen the Loch Ness monster if it had come out of the sea. I mean, I know the Loch Ness monster doesn't live in the sea but ... you know what I mean, they were ... they only had eyes for each other. Really romantic.'

The detective suddenly remembered that he was telling this story to the woman's husband and he stopped. He looked at Tom. Tom's head was down. The detective could not see if Tom was crying or not but he suddenly felt really sorry for him. He wanted to reach out his hand and touch Tom. He remembered what it felt like to find out you were losing the person you loved and in that moment the detective thought: 'this is not the job for me'.

'And then?' Tom asked. He did not want to hear any more and yet at the same time he wanted the detective to finish the story. He had to know everything.

'They ran back to the car and drove back to Boddington,' the detective said. 'They parked in front of a small building with six flats in it. They took the bags from the car and went up to the front door. She opened the door with a key and they went in.'

'*She* opened the door?' Tom asked in surprise.

'Yeah, I checked with the neighbours,' the detective replied. 'It's her flat. He was just the latest visitor. They'd seen him a couple of times but there were others before him. He was just the latest one.'

Chapter 9 *Do not use the toilet while the train is in the station*

Tom got on the train home and sat on the first free seat he came to. There were other people already sitting around the table but he did not see them. He fell into the seat, and let his case fall on the table, together with the envelope the detective had given him. The conversation with the detective was still going on in his head.

'He was just the latest one,' the neighbours had told the detective. Tom shook his head and said aloud, 'the latest one?'

The woman opposite him on the train said, 'Sorry, what did you say?' But Tom just shook his head at her and returned to his thoughts. How long had this been going on? Was this possible? He had not noticed anything . . .

Well, that was not quite true. He knew that Marina was not happy, that she was finding it difficult to get used to living in the country. But it was only with this story of the Ironing Man that he had begun to worry about her. Now it was already too late, she had found someone else because *he* had not had any time to give her.

'Oh God, I've been so stupid!' he said aloud.

The woman opposite looked at him again.

Maybe it was not too late. He loved Marina and he was sure she still loved him. But maybe she did not love him any more, maybe this 'latest one' had become important to her. 'Latest one'. 'A flat in Boddington?' This was not possible. How could she lead a double life like this without him knowing? Had he really been so busy in his work that he had just not seen what was going on? This was not like Marina. To do something and not tell him about it. No, this was not like Marina. Could she have done this? Did she feel so unloved?

The ticket inspector arrived and Tom had to look for his ticket. He pulled it out of his pocket together with his notebook. Actually he had two notebooks in his pocket and, after the inspector had seen his ticket, Tom began to look through the older notebook. It was for last year. He started at the back of the book and began to read through it, back to front. Marina's name was everywhere. Sometimes under 'Bad':

I got really angry with Marina last night. How can she spend so much time talking away on the phone! Talking about nothing!

But most often her name was under 'Good'. Lots of 'we talked late', lots of 'we went to that little Greek restaurant again tonight'. Lots of 'we . . .' On one day, her birthday two years ago, he had written eighteen things under 'Good', all about Marina. Fourteen of them were about the presents he had bought her. Like this:

Marina loved the scarf
Marina loved the earrings
Marina loved the dinosaur
Marina loved . . .

The other things were about Marina waking up to find the bedroom full of candles, a cake and a birthday card as big as the television. And about their love-making.

Tom put the notebook down on the table. What was going to happen now? Would there be another birthday for them to enjoy together? Could he still show her that he loved her? Would she take him back? He saw the envelope sitting on the table. The detective had given it to him just before Tom got on the train. Tom looked at it.

'I don't know if you'll want to look at these at all,' the detective had said.

Tom had taken the envelope from the detective who by this time looked as unhappy as Tom did.

'I'm so sorry I had to tell you all this,' the detective continued. 'I just wish . . . ' He had not finished.

Tom now sat looking at the envelope. Photographs? Yes, it must be photographs. Tom did not want to look and yet he picked up the envelope. He held it in his hand. He looked towards the open window and for a moment thought of throwing the envelope out. But no, he had to look at them.

He opened the envelope slowly and a number of colour photographs fell on the table. He looked at them. He picked up one, then another, then another, then another. A man getting out of a car. A man kissing a young woman. A couple walking on a beach, the same man and woman. The same couple in a restaurant, the same couple in front of a house. Tom did not know the man and he certainly did not know the woman.

What was going on here? Maybe the detective had given him the wrong photographs? Tom looked again at the photograph of the couple outside the first house. It was his house. It was their house, his and Marina's. There was no mistake. But who was this woman? Was this the woman the detective had followed? The detective had followed this woman! He had not followed Marina! He had followed this woman to the sports centre, to the restaurant, to the beach and back to the flat! He had watched this woman open the door of the flat and go in with 'her latest', not with Marina's 'latest'. He had not followed Marina to these places! He had not followed Marina anywhere!

'Yes! Yes! Yes!' Tom said aloud between his teeth and hit the envelope with his hand. The woman opposite him looked at Tom again but before he could say 'sorry' and smile she decided to hide behind her newspaper. She held it up in front of her. Tom said 'sorry' anyway.

He was so excited now he had to talk to someone, but this woman was probably not the right person. He thought of the detective. He took out his mobile phone and rang the number but there was nothing, no sound, nothing. Of course, the detective had said his mobile phone was not working.

Tom put the phone down. It rang immediately. It was the detective.

'Tom?' the detective asked. They had changed to using first names in the pub. 'Are you OK?'

'Yes, Phil, but listen,' Tom said. 'This woman in the photographs. This is the woman you followed?'

'Yes?' The detective did not understand why Tom asking him this.

'Tell me. What did she look like? Tell me what she was wearing?'

The detective did not say anything at first. He did not understand what was going on.

'Please, Phil, this is important!' Tom said.

The detective's description was very full and it matched the woman in the photograph.

Tom told the detective he was wonderful and that he loved him. The detective was surprised and then pleased when Tom explained. The detective was even more surprised when Tom offered to double his pay.

'No, I don't want any more money Tom,' the detective said. 'Use it to take Marina on a really nice holiday. I don't want the money, I'm just happy this was all a mistake. But listen, look after that girl of yours. Spend more time with her, OK? I mean, I may not be a very good detective but I know something about people, and I can see how important your Marina is for you, so don't lose her!'

'OK,' Tom replied.

'Anyway, I'm giving up this detective business. I don't like to see nice people being unhappy. I don't want to be part of that.'

'How long have you been doing it?' Tom asked. He was not really surprised to hear that this had been Phil's first job as a detective. They both promised to phone each other soon. Perhaps both of them had learnt more from this than they realised.

He put the phone down and saw that the woman was still hiding behind the newspaper. Perhaps she had heard Tom telling Phil he loved him. Tom smiled. He did not think the woman would come out from behind her newspaper. He would not see her again. He looked at the back of her newspaper and saw an advertisement.

The advertisement was for a holiday in the West Indies. It took Tom less than five minutes to ring the number and book a two-week holiday. It took him one minute to phone his boss and leave a message on the answerphone. He said that he was going on holiday and that he was leaving the job to spend more time with his wife.

It took Tom less than one minute to walk to the toilet. Surprisingly, when he got there, his mobile phone started to ring. It actually now worked in the toilet! But he didn't want to answer it. He wanted some peace and quiet. So he let it fall into the toilet. The phone continued to ring but more quietly. Then it disappeared onto the railway lines as Tom pressed the button above the toilet. For a few seconds he could still hear it ringing and then nothing at all.

Chapter 10   *On the beach*

Tom and Marina had been on holiday for a week now and were feeling very relaxed and very much in love. They had spent the long flight to Barbados telling each other their side of the story. Marina told Tom about Tracy and the massage and her day in London with the Ironing Man. Tom had told Marina about Phil the detective and the 'wonderful case of the wrong woman'. They had both laughed a lot and this laughter was helped by the flight assistant. She thought Tom and Marina were on their honeymoon and returned again and again to offer them more and more champagne.

'So who was this Ironing Man?' Tom asked. 'Where did he come from?'

'I have no idea,' Marina said. 'Maybe it was all in my head.'

Tom thought about this for a while.

'Well, what about the photographs of Tracy? She wasn't just in your head and she said the Ironing Man sent her, so . . .' he said.

'Does it matter? He helped us, didn't he? That's all that matters,' Marina replied.

'Yeah, you're right,' Tom said.

On the second day – they had slept most of the first day after the long journey and the champagne – Tom had taken a piece of paper and had written 'things to do' at the top of the page. He then looked up at Marina, smiled, made a ball of the paper and threw it into the toilet in their bathroom. He was becoming good at throwing things down toilets. First the mobile phone on the train and now the piece of paper.

Since then they had made no plans at all. They had done things as they felt like it, and they had done nothing when they felt like it. They had done all of this together and now they felt like a walk on the beach. The beach was empty as the sun had already set and most of the other visitors had already returned to the hotel. Tom and Marina felt they had the beach all to themselves.

Suddenly Tom stopped walking and looked along the beach. He could just see a small group of people sitting together, looking out at the sea and laughing. There were three people, two men and a woman. One of the men was quite big and for a moment Tom thought he knew him. He could not be sure because the man was not wearing a dirty, white raincoat, but he did look a little like Phil, the detective. The second man was good-looking and tall. Tom turned towards Marina and saw that she was also looking along the beach at the same group of people.

'Are you OK?' Tom asked.

'Oh yes, I'm fine. I'm very, very fine,' she said as she put her hands around his neck and pulled him into a long kiss.

When Tom and Marina finished the kiss they looked up the beach but the group of people had left. Marina turned again to Tom.

'It's just ... did you hear that woman's laugh, that blonde woman? It sounded a bit ... it sounded a bit like Tracy. And the tall man looked a bit like ... but no. That's not possible, that's not possible. Is it?'